Fantastic Sports

Mountain
BIKING

BRANT RICHARDS

ALADDIN/WATTS
LONDON • SYDNEY

This edition printed in 2000
© Aladdin Books Ltd 1998

Designed and produced by
Aladdin Books Ltd
28 Percy Street
London W1P 0LD

ISBN 0 7496 3890 7 (paperback)

First published in Great Britain
in 1998 by
Aladdin Books/Watts Books
96 Leonard Street
London EC2A 4XD

Editor
Sarah Levete

Design
David West
Children's Book Design

Designer
Flick Killerby

Illustrators
Catherine Ward (Simon
Girling & Associates)
Rob Shone

Picture Research
Brooks Krikler Research

This title was previously published
in hardcover as The Fantastic Fold-
out Book of Mountain Biking

ISBN 0 7496 3101 5 (hardback)

Equipment supplied by Trek UK
and Yellow Jersey, London

The author, Brant Richards, is an
experienced mountain bike rider
and editor of a mountain bike
magazine.

Printed in Belgium

A CIP catalogue entry for this book
is available from the British Library.

CONTENTS

Introduction

Millions of people, of all ages, enjoy the thrill and freedom of riding on a mountain bike. A mountain bike makes it easy to speed up, and down, even the steepest hills and to ride over the bumpiest terrain, or ground. From riding along a muddy trail with friends to downhill racing, riding a mountain bike offers it all – fresh air, fitness and fun.

To begin mountain biking, all you need to do is buy or hire a mountain bike and a helmet from one of the many specialist shops, where sales assistants can help you to select the right equipment. Find a stretch of flat ground away from traffic – and read on.

Whether or not you are an experienced rider, this book tells you everything you need to know, from care of your bike to bunny-hopping over logs on the trail.

Mountain biking is brilliant fun – but it can also be demanding and dangerous. Whether you ride on quiet country roads or go "off-road" in the hills, always put safety first. This involves understanding how your bike works (*see pages 12-13*), knowing how to check it properly before every ride (*see pages 22-23*), being aware of other road or countryside users and attempting only moves which you can safely perform.

With your sense of safety and fun, put on your helmet, get on a mountain bike ...and get pedalling!

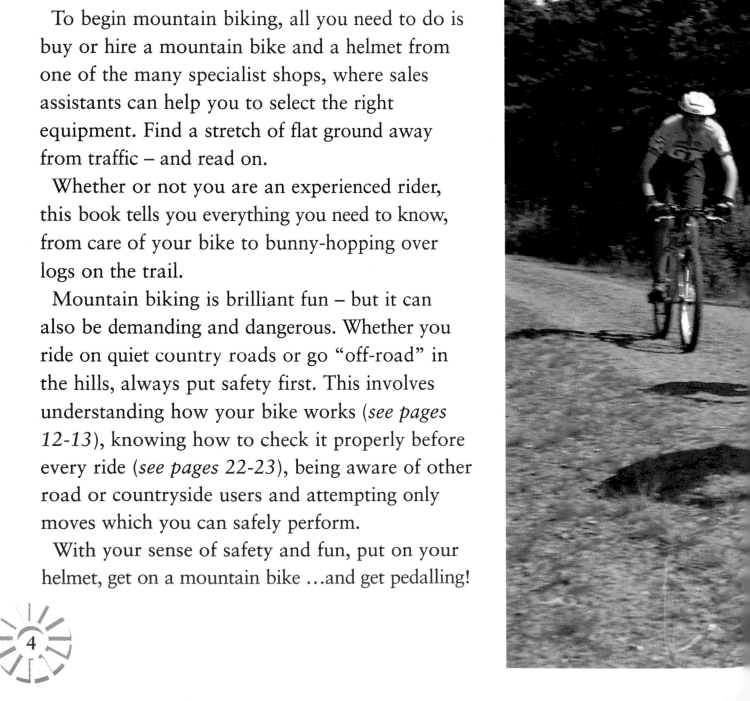

ON YOUR BIKE!

You can ride a mountain bike on city streets, or you can go "off-road", riding in the open countryside.

When you have practised the basic riding techniques (see pages 14-15), and you feel safe and confident on your bike, try out some of the different types of mountain bike riding, from riding trails (routes through the countryside, below) to tricks (see pages 26-27).

Whatever your level of riding and whatever the type of riding you are involved in, stay safe. Only attempt moves or ride distances for which you have the necessary skills and strength.

COMPETITION TIME

As a mountain biker you can simply hit the trail with a friend and just enjoy the ride, or you can take the sport more seriously (*above*), by entering different competitive events. From cross-country races to downhill races, there are events for everyone. Check out mountain biking magazines or specialist shops for up-to-date information on events which you can enter.

TIME FOR TRICKERY

Many riders enjoy the thrill of stunt riding. This involves tricks such as the "wheelie" (right). Wait until you are an experienced and skilled rider before you attempt a stunt.

Taking up
MOUNTAIN BIKING

Mountain biking is one of the most exciting sports you can enjoy. A mountain bike is often easier to ride than a regular road bike – its chunky tyres, wide range of gears and powerful brakes make it easy to cross even the roughest terrain. A mountain bike reaches the places that other bikes cannot reach, from woody tracks to steep hills.

ON THE TRAIL
When you are on a trail ride, make sure that you carry with you tools and spares for your bike.

REASONS TO RIDE
"You can just put on your helmet, get on your bike and be out in the fresh air in no time. It's a great sport for girls and boys... It's brilliant to go out on a ride with your friends... There are so many tricks to learn... It doesn't matter if you're a beginner – you can always have a good time."

Anatomy of a MOUNTAIN BIKE

A mountain bike, like any other bike, consists of a frame to which wheels and other components, such as brakes, gears and pedals, are attached.

The parts that make a mountain bike look different from other bikes are its large tyres, its set of three chainrings, which gives it low gears for hill-climbing (*see pages 14-15*), and its flat handlebars, fitted with powerful brake levers.

MOUNTAIN BIKE BRAKES

To make the brakes on a mountain bike powerful enough to stop the bike quickly and to allow the bike to be ridden through mud without jamming up, the brakes are fitted to a specially welded part of the frame.

Saddle

Seat post

Rear brake

Seat stays

Seat tube

The **front derailleur** moves the chain across the chainrings.

Rim

Sprockets

Chainrings

Chain stays

Crank

The **rear derailleur** moves the chain from gear to gear across the chainrings and sprockets (see pages 14-15), de-railing it.

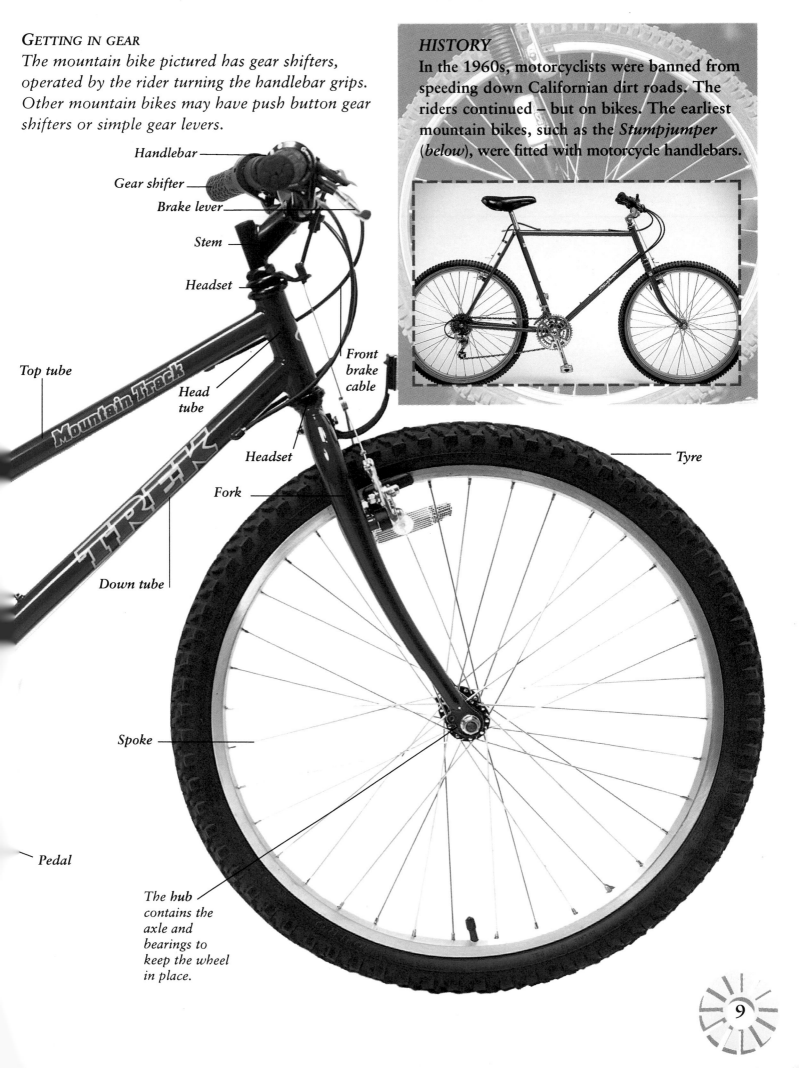

GETTING IN GEAR
The mountain bike pictured has gear shifters, operated by the rider turning the handlebar grips. Other mountain bikes may have push button gear shifters or simple gear levers.

Handlebar

Gear shifter

Brake lever

Stem

Headset

Top tube

Head tube

Mountain Track

TREK

Headset

Front brake cable

Fork

Down tube

Spoke

Pedal

The hub contains the axle and bearings to keep the wheel in place.

Tyre

HISTORY
In the 1960s, motorcyclists were banned from speeding down Californian dirt roads. The riders continued – but on bikes. The earliest mountain bikes, such as the *Stumpjumper* (*below*), were fitted with motorcycle handlebars.

Buying your MOUNTAIN BIKE

The best place to buy a mountain bike is from a specialist mountain bike shop. Here the staff will be able to advise you on which bike is the best for you – from the size of the frame, to the type of tyres that you should fit for the sort of riding you're going to be doing. They will make sure that your bike is safe to ride – you won't have to put it together yourself!

More expensive bikes are lighter and stronger, but don't think you have to spend hundreds of pounds to enjoy yourself on a bike. Whichever mountain bike you choose, you'll enjoy the ride as long as the bike is safe and right for you.

WHICH ONE?
There are literally hundreds of different bikes (above) to choose from. Ask the shop assistant to help you make the best choice.

1

2

3

WHAT DO YOU GET FOR YOUR MONEY?
The best mountain bikes can cost over £4,000, but don't worry – you can buy one much more cheaply! The type of metal used in the frame (see opposite page), *and the bike's suspension, if any, will affect the bike's price. The suspension consists of springs and pistons which absorb bumps in the ground when you ride over them. A basic, cheap mountain bike has a rigid frame, with no suspension* 1 *. A bike with front suspension* 2 *costs more, but not as much as the ultimate in comfort – a bike with front and rear suspension* 3 *.*

SIZE IS EVERYTHING!
When you choose a mountain bike to buy or to hire, it is very important that it is the right size for you.

Stand with the bike between your legs and your feet flat on the floor. Make sure that there are at least 5 cm (2 ins) between the top of your legs and the top tube of the bike, as you straddle the bike, standing near the saddle. If the distance is any less than this, it could really hurt if you came off in a crash!

Ask a sales assistant in a mountain bike shop to help make sure that the bike is suitable for your size (*left*).

IT'S ALL IN A FRAME

Mountain bike frames come in a range of different metals. These vary in strength and weight. The top-range, and most expensive, frame will be made of a very light but strong material, such as titanium (*below left*). A frame made from an aluminium alloy (*below right*) – aluminium mixed with other metals – is heavier than titanium but will be less expensive. A standard, cheap mountain bike frame is usually made from steel (*top right*). This is hard-wearing but it can be very heavy.

Don't wait!
Make sure your bike is right for you now, rather than waiting to grow into it. If you look after your bike well, you can sell it once you have outgrown it – then you will be able to buy another bike which fits you.

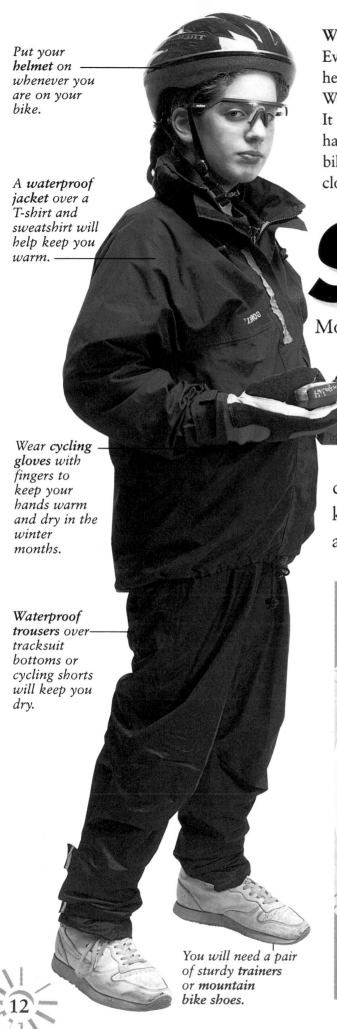

Put your **helmet** on whenever you are on your bike.

A **waterproof jacket** over a T-shirt and sweatshirt will help keep you warm.

Wear **cycling gloves** with fingers to keep your hands warm and dry in the winter months.

Waterproof trousers over tracksuit bottoms or cycling shorts will keep you dry.

You will need a pair of sturdy **trainers** or **mountain bike shoes**.

WHAT TO WEAR

Every time you ride your bike make sure you wear your helmet and that it is fastened and adjusted correctly. Wearing gloves can stop you hurting your hands if you fall. It can also stop the handlebar grips rubbing against your hands and making them sore. Wear either special mountain biking shoes or hard-wearing trainers. Remember, the right clothes will give you a more comfortable ride!

Safety and COMFORT

Mountain biking is great fun... but it can also be dangerous. Always wear the appropriate protective clothing and equipment, from gloves to a helmet. A helmet is a vital piece of equipment. Mountain biking can be an all-year-round sport, but you need different clothes for different times of the year to keep cool in warmer months (*far right*) and warm and dry in colder months (*left*).

WHY WEAR A HELMET?
If you fall off a mountain bike and hit your head hard on the ground while not wearing a helmet, you could die. Always wear a helmet. It will protect your head from injury if you crash or get knocked off your bike. When a helmet absorbs the impact of a crash, it may crack or collapse. You cannot always see a crack so you must replace your helmet after it has taken a knock.

SADDLE HEIGHT

Get your saddle at the right height – it will give you more pedal power. Ask a friend to help set the saddle height so that one of your legs is nearly straight when one of the pedals is at its lowest point (*left*). If the saddle is too low, you may be able to reach the ground more easily, but riding will be harder work. Riding with a low saddle can also damage your knees.

*A **helmet** for any weather.*

*Wear a **cycling T-shirt**, made from material to keep your body cool in the heat and warm in colder temperatures.*

TAKE CARE
Crashes can, and do, happen when you're mountain biking. But you can help prevent serious injury if you take the trouble to learn how to fall (see below) and wear the right equipment and clothing (right).

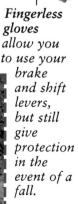

***Fingerless gloves** allow you to use your brake and shift levers, but still give protection in the event of a fall.*

***Cycling shorts** have a padded lining. Wear them without underwear to prevent chafing from the saddle.*

CRASHING SAFELY

Just in case you do crash or fall, which you may well do, it's important to know how to fall safely. If you realise you are about to crash, try to get the bike onto its side, skidding the tyres by braking to reduce the speed as much as possible. If you can, jump clear of the bike. Avoid sticking an arm out straight because this can easily lead to a painful break of your collar-bone.

Learning TO RIDE

When you have set the saddle at the correct height (*see page 13*), and you have made your pre-ride checks (*see page 23*), you can start pedalling. Find a flat area away from moving or parked cars, where you can practise operating the gears and brakes. Practise riding in circles, stopping quickly and accelerating away from a standstill using your gears to help give you more speed. When you are used to the way your bike works, or "handles", you can ride in the real world.

TAKING CORNERS
To ride a bike in a circle, don't just turn the handlebars. Lean slightly towards the direction that you want to go.
The faster you go, the more you need to lean.

SHIFTING GEARS

The range of mountain bike gears (which can be up to 24) allow you to pedal at the same rate, however steep the terrain, or ground, over which you are riding. The number of gears on your bike depends on how many chainrings and sprockets (*see pages 8-9*) there are on the bike.

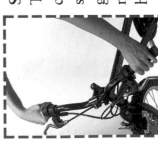

Chainrings are the cogs attached to the cranks, and sprockets are the cogs on the rear wheel. There are usually three chainrings and seven or eight sprockets.

A click or shift of your left-hand gear lever, or shifter, moves the chainrings; the right-hand gear lever, or shifter, moves the sprockets. From either of the three chainrings (low, middle and high, *see below*), you can fine-tune the gear you are in by shifting the sprockets with the right-hand gear lever.

PUT YOUR BRAKES ON!

Your mountain bike has a very powerful front and rear brake fitted to the frame (below). The brakes are operated by the brake levers on the handlebars. The left-hand lever operates the rear brake, and the right-hand lever operates the front brake. Take care when you use the front brake – if you pull too hard on it the bike may tip forwards, taking you with it! If you pull too hard on the rear brake the back wheel will skid. Try to balance the braking power between your front and rear brakes.

RULES ON THE ROAD

When you are riding on a road, ride about half a metre from the edge of the pavement, keeping clear of drains and gutters. Look ahead and take care, especially at junctions, when cars could either be pulling out or turning across you. The road is no place to practise tricks or stunts – save those for safe areas away from cars. Turn to pages 16 and 30 for further rules for riding.

PEDALLING
Keep the ball of your foot over the centre of the pedal to make pedalling easier. This will also help you to keep better control of the bike.

The high chainring on the bottom three sprockets ① is for downhill riding. The low chainring on the top three sprockets ② is for climbing hills. The middle chainring on the top three sprockets ③ is for riding on the flat.

3

2

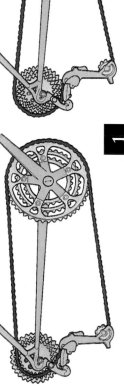

1

GEAR TIPS
❂ *Avoid changing gear when you are pedalling hard.*

Unless you are racing or riding up a steep hill, ride in the middle chainring.

15

STAY SAFE

Even when you ride in the countryside you will meet traffic, such as walkers and horse riders (above). Learn your highway code – this will help to keep you safe for town riding and off-road riding.

Where to GO RIDING

On your mountain bike, you can ride on any roads where cars are allowed. In the countryside, you can also ride on public bridlepaths – the same tracks that horses are allowed to walk on. You are not allowed to ride on public footpaths – these are for walkers only. In fact, you're not even really allowed to push your bike on footpaths! If you keep to public bridlepaths, and always give way to walkers and horses, you'll stay safe and you won't get into trouble.

Wherever you ride your mountain bike (above), always be courteous and polite to other track users.

HELP, I'M LOST!

To avoid getting lost:
❋ Ride with a responsible older rider (*right*) who knows the route.
❋ Tell your parent or carer where you are going and at what time you will be back.
❋ Never ride on your own – you could fall and no one would be able to get you help.
  If you do get lost, try to retrace your tracks until you come to a landmark which you recognise.

16

Keeping fit AND HEALTHY

Anyone can enjoy mountain biking as long as he or she is reasonably fit and healthy. You can improve your fitness by eating balanced meals (*below*) of carbohydrates (found in bread, potatoes, pasta and rice), protein (found in meat, fish, eggs, milk, cheese and pulses) and vitamins (found in fresh fruit and vegetables). If you are planning a trail of more than an hour, take along some healthy snacks and water or fruit juice (*above*).

WARMING UP

It is a good idea to warm up your muscles with a few gentle stretches (*below*) before you set off on a long ride. Stretching before and after physical activity will help to prevent your muscles from stiffening up. Your legs do a lot of work when you ride your bike. In your warm-up and cool-down (after your ride) include a stretch for your calf muscles 1 , a stretch for the front of your thighs 2 and a stretch for the back of your legs 3 .

FULL OF ENERGY
Whenever you are involved in a physical activity, such as mountain bike riding, your body loses energy. To replace this, you need to eat healthy snacks. Avoid fatty foods or foods and drinks which have lots of added sugars. These only give you a temporary burst of energy. Choose "energy bars" or snacks such as bananas or dried fruits.

1   2   3

TIM GOULD

Tim Gould (*below*) is one of the world's best mountain bikers. His speciality is hill-climbing, an event in which he has won most of the hill-climbing competitions that are put on at mountain bike races around the world. Tim Gould is also an excellent cross-country racer. Helped by his hill-climbing skills, he is better in mountainous cross-country races than those on flatter terrain.

IT'S ALL DOWNHILL!

Before you attempt to go down a steep hill you must understand how your brakes work and how to use them (*see page 15*). Just before you approach the hill, shift into a high gear (*see pages 14-15*) to give you control over your pedals. Keep your weight towards the back of the bike, to stop the bike from toppling over forwards. With your weight at the back, the front wheel is free to track over lumps and bumps. Control your speed by pumping on the rear brake. Avoid pulling on the front brake too hard, otherwise you will stop the front wheel and go hurtling over the top.

Some riders lower the saddle (see page 13) in order to keep the correct position for downhill riding, with the weight towards the rear of the bike (left).

Regular TECHNIQUES

From tackling steep hills to avoiding obstacles in your path, off-road mountain biking is full of variety! You need the techniques to meet the challenges of the terrain over which you are riding. As with any new activity, it takes patience and practice (*right*) to perfect the skill of good mountain bike riding. The more you ride, the easier it will become. Pick up some tips by watching more experienced riders.

FIRST STOP!
Stay safe by learning to stop quickly (above and see right) *before you learn to ride fast.*

IT'S ALL UPHILL!

Going up a steep hill (*right*) is a balancing act which needs lots of practice. Keep your weight over the front wheel but not so far forwards that you lose any road grip, or traction, on the rear tyre. Shift to a low gear (*see pages 14-15*) before the hill gets really steep! Crouch down to bring your upper body nearer to the handlebars than when riding on the flat. Soon, you'll be riding up slopes that some people would have difficulty walking up!

BETTER BRAKING
To stop your bike more quickly, use the front brake more. Don't pull too hard or you will fly over the handlebars. Practise stopping, using only the front brake on a flat surface. Keep the braking power even so that the wheel doesn't "lock" and slide, or throw you off the bike. Don't try this going downhill at speed.

19

Advanced TECHNIQUES

The more you ride, the more you can improve your basic techniques so that your ride is faster, more comfortable and more controlled.

For advanced moves, such as the bunny-hop, develop the ability to transfer your weight on your bike, skilfully and smoothly. Move your weight backwards to reduce the weight on the front wheel. Move your weight forwards to lighten the weight on the rear wheel. To alter the amount the bike leans when you take a corner, transfer your weight from side to side.

Soon you will be able to make the bike do anything you want!

JUMPS
Hitting a small lump in the trail can lift the bike in the air. Jumping is great, but because the bike is in the air, you're in more danger of hurting yourself. Start with small jumps; only progress to larger ones when you are confident. When you land, bend your arms and legs to reduce the impact of the bike as it lands.

CORNERING AT SPEED
To corner at speed, as shown in the sequence (*right*), keep the leg and pedal on the outside of the turn in a downwards position. Keep the leg on the inside of the turn away from the pedal, ready to put it down in case you lean over too far.

Professional riders "drift", or skid, through corners, steering in the opposite direction to control a skid with both wheels sliding sideways, and applying the brakes. It's dramatic – but best left to the professionals!

THE BUNNY-HOP

The bunny-hop allows you to lift both wheels clear of the ground at the same time. To look at it, you'd think it was impossible, but it's not! It is a useful move, especially if you come across a log or a pothole on the trail.

Begin with a single-wheel bunny-hop. Ride at a walking pace; crouch down and pull back on the handlebars as you push down on the pedals.

As you do this, the front wheel will lift off the ground. Shift your weight forwards, pushing down on the handlebars. This will lift the back wheel off the ground as the front wheel clears the obstacle. As you land, start to pedal.

For the double-wheel bunny-hop (above sequence), stay out of the saddle and crouch down. Pull on the handlebars and jump or spring the bike clear of the obstacle. Not easy, but practice makes perfect.

ALL PUMPED OUT

Mountain bike riding is hard work – for your tyres! At some point, your bike will get a puncture (below). Be prepared!

Always carry a pump, a spare inner tube, a small set of tools and a puncture repair kit

when you go for rides. Being able to mend a puncture on the trail will save you from having to push your bike home, which is not much fun. Many puncture repair kits come with easy-to-follow instructions.

IN THE WORKSHOP

It's useful to have a place such as a corner of a garage or spare room to mend (*below*), clean, maintain and adjust your mountain bike (*left*). First ask your parents or carer if you can use the room! Cover the floor with card to stop any oil or mud damaging the carpet. Store your tools neatly, cleaning them after use. Get a small tool-box to keep your tools in, and try to buy things, such as brake blocks and oil, before you need them.

Turn your bike upside down; spin the wheel to check that it is "true" – not wobbly.

Check that the quick-release lever for the rear wheel is not loose.

ALL OILED-UP

Bicycle chain oil is designed to make the chain run quietly and to stop it wearing out quickly (right). It's best to use a proper mountain bike oil. Keep it away from your brakes – even if they squeak!

TOOLS FOR THE JOB

Your bike doesn't require a huge workshop to keep it running. All you need to give your bike a long and healthy life is a selection of spanners, Allen keys, a screwdriver and a can of cycle oil – and a small booklet on bike maintenance.

* Are the gears working?
* Are the handlebars secured firmly?
* Is the saddle at the correct height?

CHECK IT OUT... REGULARLY
Every month, check these points:
* Are the chain and the gear cables well oiled? This will keep the bike running smoothly.
* Have the brake pads worn away? If so, make sure you replace them.

* *SAFETY FIRST* *
Don't work on your bike, especially your brakes, without having a responsible adult to check them for you afterwards. Loose or badly adjusted parts could cause an accident.

CHECK IT OUT... BEFORE YOU RIDE
Before you ride your bike check these points:
* Are the tyres inflated properly (*above left*)?
* Do the brakes work?
* Are the wheels fixed tightly into the frame?

Care and
REPAIR

Hold the front wheel between your legs. Rock the handlebars from side to side to check they are not loose.

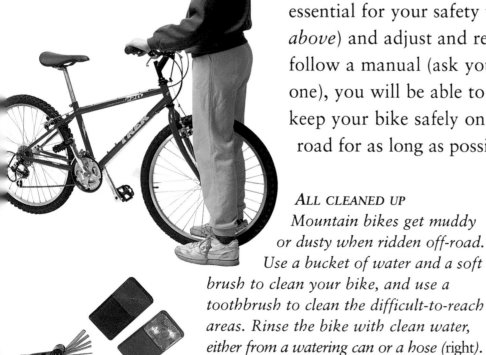

A regular care and repair check, and a clean, will keep your bike in good working order. Some parts of your bike, such as the brake blocks, wear out with use. It is essential for your safety that you check your bike (*see above*) and adjust and replace parts as necessary. If you follow a manual (ask your bike shop to recommend one), you will be able to keep your bike safely on the road for as long as possible.

ALL CLEANED UP
Mountain bikes get muddy or dusty when ridden off-road. Use a bucket of water and a soft brush to clean your bike, and use a toothbrush to clean the difficult-to-reach areas. Rinse the bike with clean water, either from a watering can or a hose (right). Oil the chain to prevent it from rusting.

Carry lights, a set of bike tools and a puncture repair kit (left) with you.

Upgrading your MOUNTAIN BIKE

When parts of your bike wear out, you can upgrade them, replacing them with better parts. By upgrading your bike, you can improve its performance. You will also be able to build a better bike from the one you already have, without having to start from scratch.

   With a good set of tools, you can upgrade your bike yourself, asking an adult to check it before you ride. Or, for a fee, your local mountain bike shop will be able to upgrade your bike.

Special cycling shoes have a mechanism which clips into these "clipless" pedals (left)

BRAKES
These "V" brakes (right and below left) *are more powerful than other brakes fitted to a standard mountain bike. They are a reasonable price and a good addition to any bike, although you will probably need new brake levers, too.*

WHY UPGRADE?
Replacing parts such as tyres, pedals or gears as they wear out lets you improve the specification of your bike, fine-tuning your bike for your needs.

For instance, you can choose tyres which will be most suitable for the type of terrain over which you ride. If you ride mostly on roads, then you can upgrade your bike with a smooth tyre which has a smaller diameter. If you ride mostly over muddy ground, you will be better off upgrading your bike with a tyre which has a rougher tread pattern, as shown in the bike below.

SUSPENSION FORKS
To give you a more comfortable ride over rocky terrain, suspension forks can be added to your bike. Made from aluminium, with rubber springs, they compress, or squash down, 70 mm to take the bumps out of the trail.

25

Tricks and STUNTS

When you are experienced at riding your bike, you can try some tricks and stunts.

Only attempt a trick or stunt which you are sure is within your ability. There is no point in doing a trick or stunt which is too difficult and which may result in a serious injury. Always wear a helmet and practise in a clear, safe path or area, well away from traffic, pedestrians and horse riders.

THE ENDO

An endo (*see sequence right and main picture*) is one of the few moves on a mountain bike in which the rider deliberately tips him or herself forwards to balance over the front wheel.

An endo is a controlled stop where the bike rocks forwards on the front wheel, then back onto both wheels. From a regular riding position [1], the rider moves his or her body weight towards the handlebars so that the rear wheel begins to lift [2]. The rider lifts the rear wheel higher still by pushing down on the pedals while pulling his or her weight over the rear wheel [3]. As the rear wheel lowers to the ground, the rider smoothly returns to a regular riding position [4].

Don't try this at high speed – walking speed is fine – anything faster is dangerous.

1

2

3

4

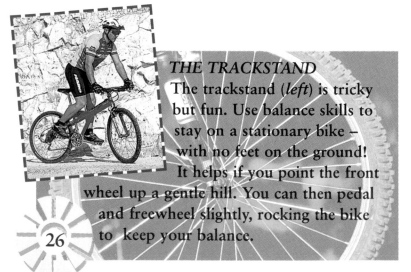

THE TRACKSTAND
The trackstand (*left*) is tricky but fun. Use balance skills to stay on a stationary bike – with no feet on the ground! It helps if you point the front wheel up a gentle hill. You can then pedal and freewheel slightly, rocking the bike to keep your balance.

THE WHEELIE

By pedalling hard in a medium gear (see pages 14-15), while pulling back on the handlebars, it's possible to lift the front wheel off the ground, as in the first step for the bunny-hop (see pages 18-19). If you can do this and keep pedalling – then you're doing a wheelie! As well as good balance skills (see page 19), a good wheelie (above), depends on the rider being able to transfer his or her weight smoothly while pedalling evenly.

27

THE SWITZERLAND SQUEAKER

No one is sure why this trick is called the Switzerland Squeaker, but it is definitely one of the most difficult tricks around. The rider does an endo (*see page 26*), but then moves his or her feet onto the front tyre (*above*). He or she then pedals the bike backwards by moving his or her feet on the front wheel. Really good riders do this trick without a rear wheel (*left*) – even harder! This is definitely not one to try at home – but it is good to know how the professionals do it:

❋ The rider removes his or her rear wheel.

❋ He or she applies the front brake.

❋ The rider places his or her feet on the front tyre.

❋ The bike rolls backwards as the rider uses the front brake for balance.

❋ **NEVER ATTEMPT ANY OF THESE STUNTS.**

HANS RAY
This German-born American rider (*right*) was the first person to develop mountain bike trick riding. Hans Ray began riding on small BMX-wheeled bikes before he began trying out an amazing range of tricks and stunts on mountain bikes. Today, Hans Ray rides professionally for a mountain bike team called Team GT. As well as competing and giving displays around the world, Hans Ray helps to develop and improve the design of sturdy mountain bikes.

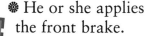

Professional tricks
AND STUNTS

These are some of the tricks that only professional stunt-riding mountain bikers can do. NEVER attempt to do these tricks yourself – leave them to the professionals. Many of these tricks developed from BMX display routines, but are now performed by mountain bikers on their larger bikes.

Top stunt riders specialise in certain skills, such as distance wheelie or bunny-hopping competitions in which the rider repeats the trick many times along a course.

THESE STUNTS ARE FOR PROFESSIONAL RIDERS ONLY. NEVER ATTEMPT THEM YOURSELF.

LOOK – NO HANDS!
If you think a normal wheelie is difficult, imagine trying to do a wheelie without using your hands! Top riders can wheelie with one hand, and some with no hands at all, by balancing the bike simply with the weight of their bodies.

This isn't the sort of trick that's any use for riding a bike but it is fun to watch. Remember though – don't try it yourself. Stunt riders have trained for years so they can perform these tricks safely.

From a standard wheelie (see page 27), a stunt rider moves smoothly into a no-hander wheelie (above and right).

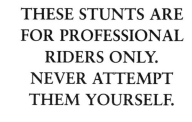

29

Have fun STAY SAFE!

Your mountain bike is a great way to keep fit, to have fun and to see the countryside – but you must always be aware of safety. Have a pre-ride check and regularly maintain your bike (*see pages 22-23*). Only attempt moves for which you have the right skills and always follow the on-and off-road rules (*see page 15 and below right*). Take a basic first-aid kit (*right*) with you on long rides. You can seriously injure yourself, or someone else, if you take unnecessary risks. Remember, enjoy yourself... and take care out there.

FIRST-AID
Don't move a person who has had a bad crash. He or she may have a back or neck injury which can result in paralysis if the person is moved. Leave one member of your group with them and send someone for help.

As well as your lights, helmet and some refreshments, you will need to take along with you a sense of humour! You may well get very muddy (below) *and wet – enjoy it!*

BE SEEN
If you think you may be out on your bike when it gets dark, take your lights (*left*). Check before you leave that the lights are working. It is a good idea to take with you a set of spare batteries. Wear a bright reflective strip to help other people see you – on and off the road.

MOUNTAIN BIKE RULES

❀ Always wear a helmet.
❀ Respect other road and trail users.
❀ Make sure your bike is well maintained and safe.
❀ Only ride where you can legally do so.
❀ Don't "trick ride" on roads.
❀ Carry tools, a puncture kit and a first-aid kit with you.
❀ Always tell your parent or carer where you are going.
❀ Try to travel in a group.
❀ TAKE CARE AND HAVE FUN!

Mountain Bike Words

BMX A bicycle, with small wheels, designed for stunts, tricks and racing.

Brakes The movement of the brake lever pushes the brake pad onto the rim of the tyre, slowing down and stopping the bike.

Bunny-hop A trick which involves "jumping" the bike off the ground.

Cable A length of wire that controls the gears and brakes.

Chainrings The cogs at the front of the bike driven or turned by the gears and chain.

Chain set A term used for the cranks and chainrings.

Clipless pedals Pedals without toe clips but to which special bike shoes can be attached.

Cogs Small "teeth" at the front and rear of the bike which are driven by the movement of the gears and the chain.

Crank The arm which attaches the pedal to the chain.

Cross-country racing A race which goes over a variety of tracks and terrains.

Downhill racing A race which goes downhill only.

Endo A trick in which the rider tips forwards over the front wheel, without falling off.

Frame The collection of tubes which are welded together to form the main part of the bike.

Freewheeling Riding without pedalling.

Gears The chain moves from gear to gear across the chainrings and sprockets. In a low gear, the wheel spins more slowly to every turn of the pedal. In a high gear, the wheel spins faster to every turn of the pedal.

Grips The rubber covers which are fitted onto the handlebars.

Headset Contained within the head tube, the bearings in which the fork tube rotates.

Hub The part of the bike which contains the axle and bearings.

Off-road Any riding which is not on a road.

Rim The part of the wheel which the tyre sits on.

Shifters The levers on the handlebars which allow you to change gear.

Sprockets The cogs at the rear of the bike, driven or turned by the movement of the chain.

Suspension The part of the bike which is supported by a spring which moves when it is hit by a bump.

Terrain The ground over which you ride.

Toe clips Attachments on the pedal, used with a toe strap, to help secure the foot to the pedal.

Traction The grip which the tyre has on the road.

Trail A trail is an off-road track over which you ride.

Trail riding Riding distances over hills or off-road.

Tread The pattern on the tyre which helps to grip the road.

Trials A competitive event in which riders perform stunts.

Upgrades New and improved parts to add to a bike.

Wheelie A trick in which you ride with the front wheel off the ground.

Index

Photo Credits: *Abbreviations: t-top, m-middle, b-bottom, r-right, l-left*

All the pictures in this book are by Steven Behr of Stockfile apart from the following pages: back cover – Frank Spooner Pictures; 4-5, 8-9, 10 all, 11l & inset, 12t & b, 13t & r, 14b, 17tl, 17ml all, 17b all, 22-23m, 23t inset, 23bl, 24-25, 25tl, 25m & 30t – Roger Vlitos; 6tr & 18m – Bob Allen/Stockfile.

The publishers would like to thank Trek UK, Yellow Jersey, London and Steven and Jill Behr of Stockfile for their help and co-operation in the preparation of this book.